BEADED
TREASURE PURSES:
Tubular Brick Stitch Designs

by

Deon DeLange

Eagle's View Publishing Company
6756 North Fork Road
Liberty, UT 84310

ISBN: 0-943604-53-2
Library of Congress Catalog Card Number: 96-85685

FIRST EDITION

10 9 8 7 6 5 4 3 2 1

CONTENTS

Treasure Purse Designs   61

Freeform Stitch

WELCOME

About three years ago I saw a small beaded purse necklace worn by a woman who came into my shop. We talked for a while and she explained that she had made it using round peyote stitch.

I loved the looks of the little purse, but since brick stitch has been a very large part of my daily life for over 25 years, I decided that there must be a way to make such a purse using brick stitch. The challenge was on! I began to experiment, as it didn't seem it should be too difficult. I made a foundation row, joined it to form a ring, and proceeded to build a little brick stitch purse. It wasn't too long after I completed that first purse before I sold it. Then I made another, and another, etc. I started getting orders for these little purses from a nearby gallery. I made more of them, as gifts. Then I started getting little purse orders over the phone. It seemed the more I made, the more I sold. They were becoming more and more popular, and soon I noticed a few beading books and magazines were including instructions on how to make them, but they were made using stitches other than brick stitch.

People began asking me when I was going to write a book on them - **this is the result of their asking**!

My desire and purpose for this book is that it may bring you as much satisfaction, encouragement, inspiration, and pleasure making these purses as having the opportunity of sharing it with you has brought to me.

May we always find joy in using the creative talents that God has given us, and sharing our joy with others. Never tire of creating new things - it produces more and more ideas.

I encourage you to *bead on and on - and have fun with your beadwork*; don't make it hard work, enjoy what you are doing!!!

Bead On !

Deon De Lange

5

ACKNOWLEDGMENTS

I would especially like to acknowledge the following people:
BEVERLEY SIMKO - for her *Zig-Zags* design. Bev is a great friend, a good student, and a fellow beadaholic
DENISE KNIGHT - for her editing capabilities and her hard work;
DON DeLANGE - my husband, for the beautiful Copper Enamel Beads he is making - some of which I have used on various pieces throughout this book.

Thank You

First, I give continuous thanks to God for the talents and creative capabilities He has given me and the ideas that flow from these talents and abilities.

I thank my wonderful husband and best friend, Don, for his unwaivering love and support. I'm very grateful, honey. I thank you also for being patient and tolerant in allowing me to pursue my passion for beads. You are a great source of encouragement to me.

I am thankful to our children, Monique (Nikki) Rose, Yvette Quale, and Don, Jr. for their support and encouragement through all these years of talking about, looking at, and at times practically "eating, breathing, and living" beads, and at the same time continuing an interest in doing beadwork themselves. It would be unfair to not mention the following people who are also a big part of my life, and they are our children's spouses: Dale L., Dale Q., and Roxanne D. Our three grandchildren, Zachery and Alyssa Quale, and Stephen DeLange also play a big role in our lives. ALSO, THEY ARE POTENTIAL THIRD GENERATION BEADERS!!!

To my mother, Lucille Rose, goes a big "Thank You Mom", for always believing in me and in what I could do.

A huge note of gratitude and thankfulness goes to my publisher, Monte Smith, who has made it all possible for me to share with all of you the love of beads. Thank you, Monte, for your confidence in me, and for allowing me to fulfill my dream.

I especially want to thank all of you who have purchased my books, video, and kits. Thank you for allowing me to be part of your life and letting me share with you what I have learned and developed.

I would like to encourage all of you who wish to contact me to write to me c/o the Eagle's View Publishing address on the back of this book.

I welcome all comments, questions, and suggestions you may have and also any ideas, pictures, etc., (perhaps for inclusion in another book). If you would like to write just to say "hi" and correspond, please let me hear from you. Looking forward to your letters, and perhaps a picture of yourself. I have enjoyed meeting many of you in person, and would like the opportunity to meet more of you. If you are going to be in the vicinity of the Oregon Coast, please contact me through my publisher and I will contact you to make arrangements from there. Hope to meet many of you soon.

Zig-Zags

INTRODUCTION

Although beaded purses are being introduced in this book, the basic brick stitch directions that were in the first three volumes (*Techniques of Beading Earrings*, *More Techniques of Beading Earrings*, and *Techniques of Fashion Earrings*) are repeated herein for the benefit of those who do not have access to these earlier books and for those who have these books but wish to have all the material in one place.

Many of the designs used in the other three books can be adapted to making beaded purses.

Also included in this book are directions for other stitches used on various parts of the purses, such as the straps, the fringe, and the edgings. These are explained in the appropriate chapters.

Only the body of each purse is charted, and the completed purse including straps, fringe, etc. is shown in the photographs. This is to enable you to choose the various components you desire to finish your personal purse, i.e., the strap from one purse, and the fringe from another. Be creative and mix and match.

Please use your imagination to create a purse of your liking. Experiment with different color combinations, various types of beads, beading the same design on both sides of the purse, or perhaps putting a different design on each side of the same purse (just make sure your bead count will allow for each design area). Don't be limited by what you see and learn here. Try your new ideas and methods, you never know what may develop. **Remember: Mistakes are not failures, they are steps to learning. Relax and have fun!!!**

Making jewelry with beads is enjoyable and creative. There are, however, a few things to keep in mind that will help make beading easier and will also be helpful in using this book.

(1)   Be selective in choosing beads of uniform size. This is very important in this kind of beadwork in order to obtain a pleasing, over-all appearance and to ensure uniformity in design.

The most uniform beads are available from Indian craft supply houses or bead stores and are purchased in bunches called "hanks". When buying beads, it is important to place all of the colors to be used side by side and insure that all of the beads are uniform. Each hank, however, will have a number of beads that have weird shapes or are slightly larger or smaller than the others and these should be discarded as the beading is done. If it is necessary to purchase the beads in containers, be very selective about the uniformity of the beads chosen when beading.

(2)   When making any of the purses that have both bugle beads and seed beads, the size of the bugle bead determines what size seed bead to use. Therefore, **a size 3/° bugle bead may be used with size 11/° or 12/° seed beads**, but **a size 2/° may be used with only size 12/° seed beads** or smaller. In all glass seed beads **the larger the number the smaller the bead**.

(3)   Keep the beads in separate containers or jars. This will make finding the needed color and size bead easier and will ensure that different sizes do not get mixed. For future work, it may be advisable to not only label the size and color on the containers, but also the color number and where they were purchased. Most craft supply houses have their own color numbers and this will make reordering easier.

(4)   Be sure to have enough beads of the proper colors to finish a project before beginning. Bead colors will vary in shade from dye batch to dye batch and it is often impossible to find the right shade when a project is half complete.

(5)   When beading, use a felt-covered desk blotter or a piece of styrofoam that has been covered with fabric. It is best to have a work area that is comfortable to work on and that will not allow the beads to roll away. As the beading is done, the different colors and sizes of beads should be kept in separate piles, or in different saucers (white is the best color), or trays, or they may be taken directly from the hank

strings. The idea is to be able to select uniform beads while working, so try different methods to find the one that works best for you.

(6)   The best needles for this kind of work are English made, size 13/° or 15/° beading needles. Japanese needles are generally too big for beads size 11/° and smaller. A rule of thumb: If the needle package contains a needle threader, the needles are too big. The needles used should be at least one size smaller than the beads.

(7)   The best thread to use is "Nymo" (made of nylon), in size "A", "O", or "OO" for the smaller hole beads, and size "B" for larger hole beads.

The size of the bead hole will help determine what size needles and thread to use. For the purses made with Delica and size 11/° beads, size "B" thread was used; for purses made with hex beads, size 12/° cut beads, etc., a size "O" was used.

Because of the greater bead count in a purse, new pieces of thread will have to be added more often than in earrings and smaller items. This means more passes of the thread through beads to tie-off and add-on threads. Keep this in mind when selecting a thread size. Using 3 to 4 yards of thread at a time decreases the number of times a new thread must be added, but takes more control and patience when pulling the thread through (to keep it from knotting). Remember - haste makes waste. It is better to slow down a little than to have to take your work out and do it again. Stay calm.

(8)   Always work in a well lighted room. It may be that a clamp-on elbow lamp or a desk lamp with an adjustable neck will be helpful. However, fluorescent lighting is not suggested, as it tends to alter the color of some beads.

(9)   A pair of small-pointed, sharp craft scissors will be very helpful. When cutting the thread from a finished piece of beadwork, lay the scissor blades flat against the beadwork and then clip carefully close to the work. Clipping the threads with just the tips of the blades at an angle could cut threads that are part of the beadwork and should not be cut.

(10)   When making purse and earring sets, try to use complimentary designs that show a relationship between the two. A purse using

floral designs will compliment earrings if they also have similar floral designs, etc. The use of elements from the purse trimmings will have a similar effect.

(11) Please read the complete procedure for making a particular purse, strap, etc., before beginning the beadwork so that you will have a more complete understanding of the technique.

(12) If a piece of beadwork is troublesome and just doesn't seem to be cooperating (dangles uneven, even though the bead count is correct; thread twisting, catching on everything possible, or knotting up, etc.) and the tension builds because mistakes keep happening, here's a suggestion - Put It Down and walk away for a while. Come back later, refreshed and relaxed, and try again.

(13) Try alternating work on simple designs with work on more elaborate, time-consuming projects. Making something familiar and not very "involving" will give a sense of relief from deep concentration and frustration. Make beadwork fun and frivolous, as well as challenging, and your enthusiasm level will stay high.

(14) When working with transparent beads, using black thread instead of white thread will make the color a darker shade. Black thread will also enhance the coloration of iridescent transparent beads, both colored and crystal types.

(15) Change the appearance of beadwork patterns by using various dangle styles and by using different types of beads in the dangles. Experiment with long bugles, porcupine quills, and various sized/shaped accent beads at the bottom of the dangles.

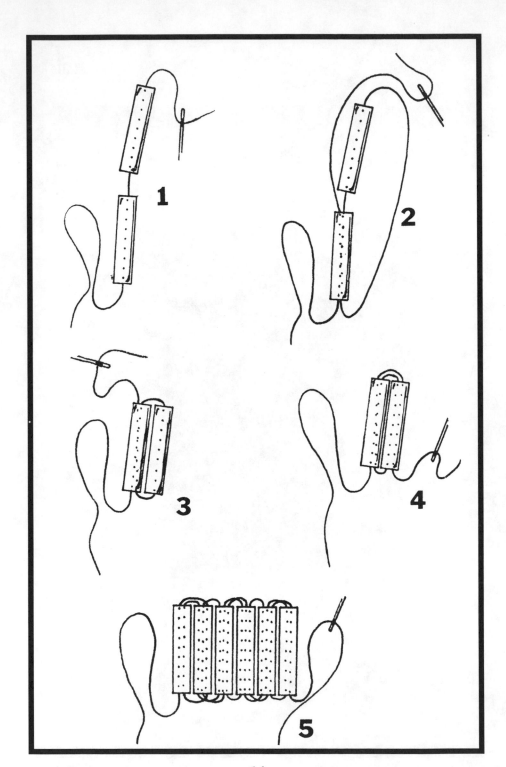

DEON'S DESIGNS ORIGINALE

This first section explains the basic techniques of Brick Stitch. Bugle Beads are the foundation for the simplest form of Brick Stitch and serve as a starting point. The number of beads in the foundation determines the width and the overall size of the finished piece. Seed bead foundations and multiple bead units are also explained.

BRICK STITCH DIRECTIONS

PHASE I

This phase will form the foundation row of bugle beads to which the rest of the piece is attached. Count the number of bugle beads in the chosen design and join them as follows:

STEP 1 - Using a single thread (just over two (2) yards long for an earring six (6) bugle beads wide), place two (2) bugle beads on the thread and push them to within 6-8" of the end (leave enough thread to tie off later), as shown in **Figure 1**.

Holding the short thread down, make a clockwise circle with the needle and go "up" through the first bugle bead following the direction of the thread (**Figure 2**). Pull the thread tight, and the two bugles will come together parallel with each other (**Figure 3**).

The needle will now be coming "up" through the first bugle bead. Complete this step by placing the needle "down" through the second bead (**Figure 4**).

STEP 2 - Continue adding bugle beads, one at a time, following the procedure described above and shown in Figures 2 through 4.

Notice that there is a rhythm to this procedure as it progresses. The thread will go in a clockwise direction and then in a counterclockwise direction, then clockwise again, etc.

As bugle beads are added, make sure that the thread is coming either up through, or down through the last bugle bead, depending upon the direction the thread is going. This can be simplified by **always** keeping the short "beginning" thread facing toward the left and downward (**Figure 5**). This will help lessen any confusion and assist in keeping the proper place.

When the beading thread is in the last bugle bead strung, pick up another bugle bead and, following the course of the thread, go either up through or down through the last attached bugle. For example, if there are two (2) bugle beads attached, the thread will be coming down through bugle number 2. Put bugle number 3 on the needle and go back down through bugle #2. Now go up through bugle #3. Put on bugle number 4 and follow the thread by going back up through bugle #3, then down through bugle #4, and so on.

As shown in Figure 5, the rhythm for a six (6) bugle bead-wide piece will be: Bugles #1 and #2 on the thread (with short thread to the left and pointing down), then up through #1, down through #2 and add number 3; down through #2, then up through #3 and add number 4; up through #3, then down through #4 and add number 5; down through #4, then up through #5 and add number 6; up through #5 and down through #6.

With all six bugles in place, **work the thread back across the bugles to reinforce them**. This is done by going up through #5, down through #4, up through #3, down through #2 and up through #1.

When the required number of bugle beads are in place, **do not cut the thread**. The next phase is the upper portion of the beadwork piece. To begin **the thread should always be coming "up" through the first bugle bead** before adding the seed beads. Therefore, the first small bead should always be on the left side of the piece (**Figure 6**).

PHASE II

This phase will form the top portion of the beadwork piece. It is accomplished by adding one seed bead at a time to the bugle bead foundation just completed.

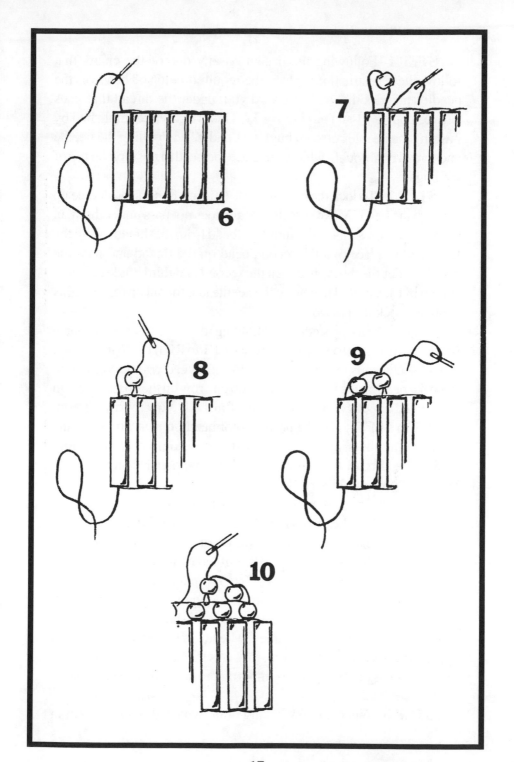

STEP 1 -Following the design on any one of the charts that follow these instructions, place the required color of bead on the needle and pass the needle toward you, under the thread that goes between bugle #1 and #2 (**Figure 7**). This is easily accomplished by pushing the needle between bugles #1 and #2 and pulling the needle and thread on through, which will place the bead in position on top of the bugles.

STEP 2 - To lock the bead in place (**Figure 8**) pass the needle up through the bead. Make sure the needle does not pass under the span of thread again as this will remove the bead from the thread. With the first bead in place, put the second bead on the thread and pass the needle under the thread between the second and third bugle beads as shown in **Figure 9**. Then bring the needle and thread up through this bead and lock it in place.

Continue this procedure (following the colors on the chart), beading on the first row of beads from LEFT to RIGHT. With the first row of seed beads in place, the needle and thread will be coming up from the bead on the far right. Move up one row on the charted design to the bead directly above the row just finished. Now following from RIGHT to LEFT, place the proper color beads, one at a time, on the thread using the same procedure as the preceding row, but **going under the thread between the seed beads**, rather than the bugle beads as shown in **Figure 10**.

The work on the seed bead portion (Phase II) will continue in a LEFT to RIGHT, then RIGHT to LEFT, then LEFT to RIGHT, etc., manner. As this proceeds there will be one less bead in each row added. Also, the first row of beads will have one less bead than the bugle bead row (see **Figure 11**). Therefore, a piece of beadwork containing seven (7) bugle beads in the foundation row (Phase I), will have six (6) seed beads in the first row, five (5) beads in the next row, four (4) beads in row three, three (3) beads in the next row and two (2) seed beads in the fifth, or top, row. As the beading is done in this phase, it is easy to see why it is important to use beads that are all the same, exact size.

STEP 3 - When the row having only two beads has been put in place, it is time to add the hanging loop: After locking the last bead in place on the top row, the thread will be coming up out of the bead on the right side in this example of seven bugle beads wide. However, using an even number of bugle beads will result in ending with the thread on the left side. As shown in **Figure 12**, place an even number of beads on the thread (approximately six (6) beads for earrings), go through these beads again and then take the needle down through the other bead on the two-bead or top row. Now pull the loop next to the top row.

In larger pieces, as the loop that has been formed will support the piece, work the thread through the same beads again (including the beads in the loop). This will add strength.

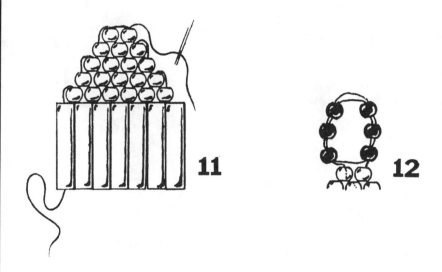

11

12

PHASE III

In this phase the bead dangles will be put in place at the bottom of the beadwork piece.

To do this, work the thread, diagonally, down through the beads to the bugle bead at the starting point as shown in **Figure 13**. With the thread down through the first bugle bead on the left, place the appropriate number and colors of seed beads on the thread (following the chart for the correct number and colors). Add one bugle bead at the bottom of the dangle, as indicated on the charts, and add three (3) seed beads. With the exception of these last three seed beads, pass the needle back up through all of the beads on the dangle; then push the needle back up through the first bugle on the foundation (Phase I) row as shown in **Figure 14**.

Adjust the dangle so that it will hang properly by placing a finger tip over the center bead of the three beads at the bottom of the dangle. By pulling the thread, adjust the dangle so that it hangs properly without too much or too little tension. As the work progresses, it is possible to feel the proper amount of tension.

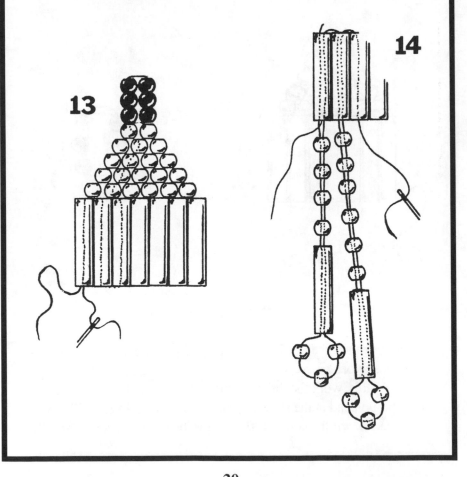

To progress to the next dangle, pass the needle down through the next bugle bead on the foundation row (bugle bead #2), and add the next beaded dangle following the chart for color and number of beads.

Continue this process until all of the dangles are in place. Make sure that each has been properly adjusted so that they all hang with the same amount of tension.

PHASE IV

As shown in **Figure 15**, when the dangles have been put in place, tie the thread off between two of the rows of seed beads on the outside edge in the top portion of the piece. As shown in **Figure 16**, every other row of beads has a thread on the outside edge and it is desirable to tie two knots just above one of these beads. This way, the thread knots will lie between the beads and when the thread is passed up through additional beads to be concealed, the knot will pull snug against the bead and be less noticeable.

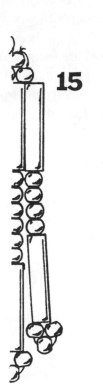

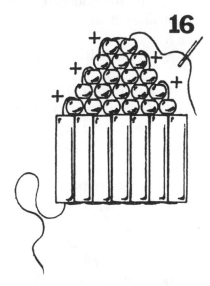

When the thread has been concealed in additional beads, clip it off close to the beads, holding the scissors flat against the beadwork. It is suggested when concealing the thread that, after knotting, the thread be woven through beads on the inner part of the beadwork before it is clipped off to ensure that the knot does not slip.

After completing this step, thread the short beginning thread on the needle and tie it off in the same manner as just described above - working the thread through a few beads, after knotting, to conceal it.

MULTIPLE BEADED STYLES

Seed Bead Foundations

Seed beads may also be used in Phase I. Units of one (1) to four (4) seed beads (or more) are used in place of bugle beads to form the foundation row. This is shown in **Figures 17 through 22**, where units of three seed beads are used in place of each bugle bead (as an example). The complete instructions for Phase I are found on pages 15-16. If more than four beads are used in a single unit, gaps tend to occur between the units and care must be taken to pull them together snugly. When the foundation row is complete, proceed as usual with the creation of the beadwork piece.

Multiple-Bead Unit Tops

Similar to seed bead foundations, the main difference between this technique and the basic style is the use of units of two (2) or more seed beads in place of the single seed beads in Phase II. The steps are exactly the same as on pages 16-19, except that two (or more, depending on the design) seed beads are placed on the thread each time instead of one seed bead (see **Figure 22**). When the top portion is complete, proceed as usual with the creation of the beadwork.

When making a design with a foundation row that has two or more seed beads per unit and two or more colors, be sure to read the graph in the same direction that the thread is going. If the thread is

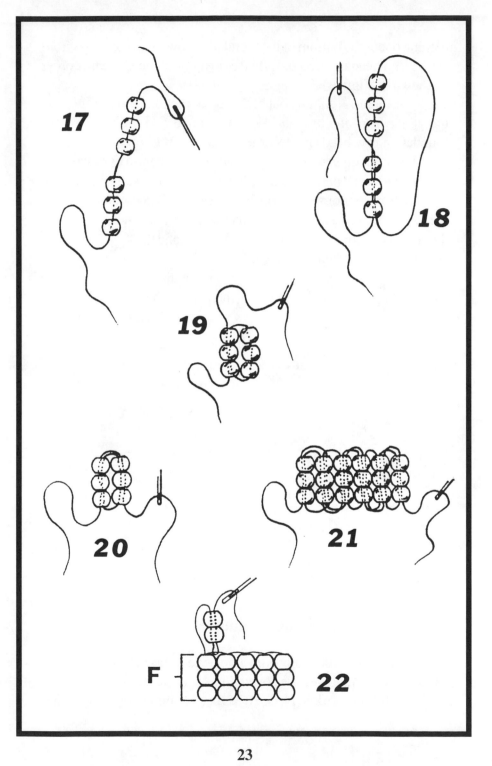

coming out of the bottom of the foundation row, read the graph from the bottom bead upward and add the next unit of beads in this order as shown in **Figure 23**.

If the thread is coming out of the top of the foundation row, read the graph from the top bead downward and add the next unit of foundation row beads in this order as shown in **Figure 24**.

The direction in which the graph is read (either up or down) will change with each unit of beads in the foundation row. For example: top to bottom, bottom to top, top to bottom, etc. Please note that when the top portion of a design has units of two or more seed beads, the thread always comes out of the top of the row and the graph is always read from the top bead downward.

Get in the habit of reading graphs in this manner, because, although it is not always necessary, there are some designs in which reading the graph as explained is crucial to creating the design correctly.

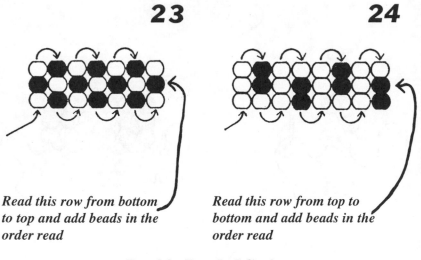

23 **24**

Read this row from bottom to top and add beads in the order read

Read this row from top to bottom and add beads in the order read

Double-Beaded Styles

This is an exceptionally attractive style of brick stitch and all of the techniques involved are covered in the basic steps.

After the top portion (Phase II) has been completed, turn the piece upside down and repeat the steps in Phase II on the other side of the foundation row. However, on this bottom portion, the beading will include a one-bead row. It may be helpful to turn the graph upside down while beading this section. Now the dangles may be added.

Starting at the one-bead row, add the appropriate number and color of beads to form the first bottom dangle. Take the needle back up through the bottom bead and then work the needle up until it comes out on the right side of the piece, just below the outside bead in the three-bead row. Add the beads for the next dangle and go up through this outside bead (**Figure 25**). Then work up until the needle is just below the outside bead, on the right-hand side of the five-bead row. Continue until there is a dangle on every other bottom row on the right-hand side. Work over to the left-hand side and add the corresponding dangles on this side.

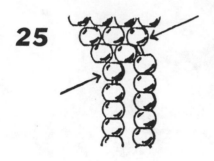

25

When all of the dangles are in place, tie the thread off as described in Phase IV (pages 21-22).

Adding Thread

When working on larger pieces of beadwork it may be necessary to add thread to the project. When the thread being used reaches about 6 to 8" in length, tie it off as described in Phase IV. To add a new length of Nymo, run the new thread through a few beads over to the edge of the beadwork and tie two knots using the same method as when the old thread was tied off. When the new thread is tied in, weave it up to the point where the beading was left off and continue as usual until the piece is complete. Figure 16 (page 21) indicates the best places to tie off and/or add the new thread.

26

TUBULAR BRICK STITCH PURSE INSTRUCTIONS

CHARTING

Tubular brick stitch is worked in the same manner as basic brick stitch, with the exception that in tubular brick stitch **all the rows contain the same bead count**. This is accomplished by deciding on the design pattern to be used, and then charting it for brick stitch as follows:

(1) The **total bead count for the foundation row in a tubular piece using brick stitch will be twice the number required for a pattern used in a single thickness flat piece**, as it accounts for both sides of the piece. For instance, a design that is 24 across the foundation row in a flat piece will be 48 for the tubular piece.

(2) The **total bead count for the entire foundation row must be an even number of beads** in order for the foundation row of beads to match up when closing the bottom of a purse. Any design or pattern for a regular flat piece of brick stitch will work for a purse, no matter what bead count or what size, as the bead count for the foundation row when doubled will be an even number.

(3) When charting for tubular brick stitch the edge beads on the right side of the chart should be staggered opposite the corresponding beads on the left edge of the chart in the same row. This is necessary so that there will be no gaps when the ends of the row are joined (a zipper-like effect).

To keep this simplified, **all purse charts in this book are done in the same way** (starting at the foundation row): the rows in the spaces of the graph paper have the right edge beads as the outer-most beads (referred to as "out" beads) and the left edge beads as the inner-most beads (referred to as "in" beads).

The rows on the lines of the graph paper have the right edge beads as the inner-most beads (again known as "in" beads), and the beads on the left edge as the outer-most beads (again known as "out" beads).

To begin charting, first determine the design to be used, and then use the spaces of the graph to draw in the foundation row for **the front side of the purse only** . Make sure the bead on the right edge is an "out" bead and the one on the left edge is an "in" bead.

For the next row - which will be on the lines of the graph - make sure the bead on the right edge is drawn just to the left of the first bead of the foundation row (this is an "in" bead). The bead on the left edge of this row will be an "out" bead. Chart the remaining rows in the same manner (**Figure 26**).

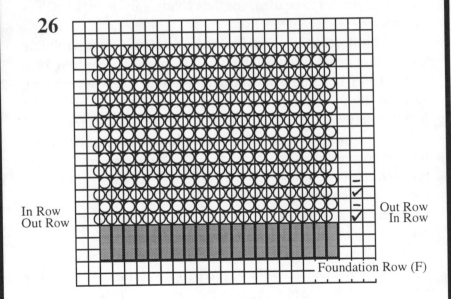

Look at the completed graphs in this book and notice that, reading from the foundation row to the top of the graph, the edge beads on the right hand side read as follows: out, in, out, in, out, in, etc. Conversely, the beads on the left hand side (reading the graph from the foundation row to the top) read as follows: in, out, in, out, in out, etc.

If a design requires that both the areas above and below the foundation row be worked in brick stitch, chart the design below the foundation row using the same "in, out, in, out, etc. method described above. Make sure the right hand bead of the first row is an "in" bead.

This sounds much more complicated than it is. Studying the charts in this book should clarify this explanation. Once this concept is grasped, it will be much easier to understand how the purses go together. It will also help when graphing your own designs or adapting other designs for tubular brick stitch. **Remember**: Only the front portions of the purses have been charted. This is to better utilize space and also to help eliminate confusion.

Some of the purses are made with various types of foundation row beads: Some with bugle beads, others using beads of another type instead of bugle beads (seed beads, delica, hex, etc.). Sometimes two or more beads are used in place of each bugle bead by stacking them. The **spaces** of the graph paper are always used to chart the foundation row. Where beads of another type that have been stacked upon each other are used, the chart uses one vertical space to represent each bead. A bugle bead is represented by three vertical spaces indicated as one bugle bead. For example, two stacked beads are indicated by two vertical spaces to represent one unit in the foundation row, three beads stacked would be indicated by three vertical spaces to represent one unit in the foundation row, etc. If single seed beads (or other type except bugle) are used in the foundation row, they are charted using only one vertical space per bead.

STEPS USED IN MAKING BEADED PURSES

(1) **Foundation Row** (see page 31)

(2) **Body of Purse** (see page 32)

(3) **Top Edge Trimmings** - optional; Picot edging, Points edging, Scallop edging, Fringe, etc. (see page 43).

(4) **Bottom Edge Trimmings** - optional; Double Beaded, Various Fringe Types, Tassels, etc. (see page 49).

(5) **Necklace Straps** - Strands, Flat Peyote, Free-form, Chevron (see pages 55 and 81).

Wabunung
(Spring Man)

FOUNDATION ROW

Decide on the design and the beads to be used and, referring to the chart, make the foundation row and reinforce it as explained in Phase I of the basic instructions for brick stitch (see pages 15-16). Make the foundation row according to the design as charted and then continue in the background color until the proper total bead count required for the particular design is reached. This establishes the working bead count for the remainder of the purse, therefore making it unnecessary to chart the back portion of the purses. The only time the back portion will require charting will be when a design is desired there. **Please Note**: only the foundation row will be made reading the chart from left to right - all other rows above the foundation row will be made reading the chart from right to left as the beading will be done in a clockwise direction. Again: Read the chart **from left to right only for the foundation row**. Read the chart **from right to left for all remaining rows above the foundation row**.

When the foundation row is completed and reinforced, form it into a ring by bringing the first bead(s) strung, where the needle and thread are, around from back to front until it meets the last bead(s) in the foundation row (as in Phase I, bugle beads are used in the illustration; if using seed beads or multiple bead units, simply substitute). Connect the two ends by passing the needle and thread down through the beads on the left edge and up through the beads to the right, then repeat a second time to securely fasten the ends together (**Figure 27**). The needle and thread will be emerging from the top of the first bead(s). The

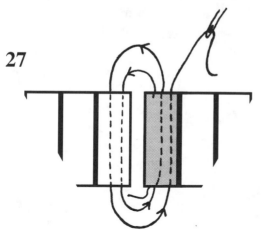

27

short portion of thread, which marks the beginning of the foundation row, will be emerging from the bottom of the same bead(s), and will be on the right hand side. This will be the starting place for each row of the purse.

When the foundation row is completed, place a "check" mark off to the right side of the chart to help keep your place (see Figure 26).

BODY OF PURSE

The **First Row** of the purse body (and all odd numbered rows above the foundation row) is charted on the lines of the graph paper and the right edge bead is an "in" bead. Remember, read the chart for this and all other rows (above the foundation row) **from right to left**!!

Work this row using the brick stitch by placing a bead of the proper color, according to the chart, above each span of thread in the foundation row. Work the uncharted portion for the back of the purse to the **left** of the charted design portion. The bead count for the uncharted portion will be the same bead count as the front portion, that is, half of the total bead count. For example, if the total bead count for the purse is 48, then the uncharted portion will be 24 beads worked in the background color. Once the total bead count is established in the foundation row, completing the uncharted portion in the remain-

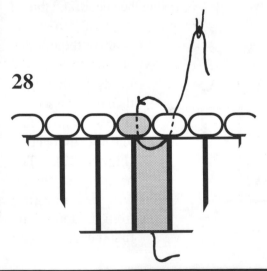

28

der of the purse is merely a matter of working in the background color until the place where the row began is reached.

When the last bead of the first row is in place, **close this row (and all odd-numbered or "in" bead rows)** by passing the needle and thread down through the first bead of this row from

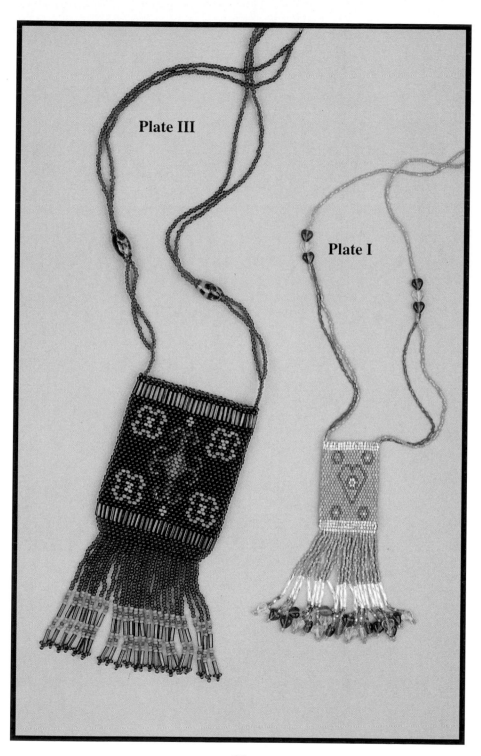

Plate III

Plate I

33

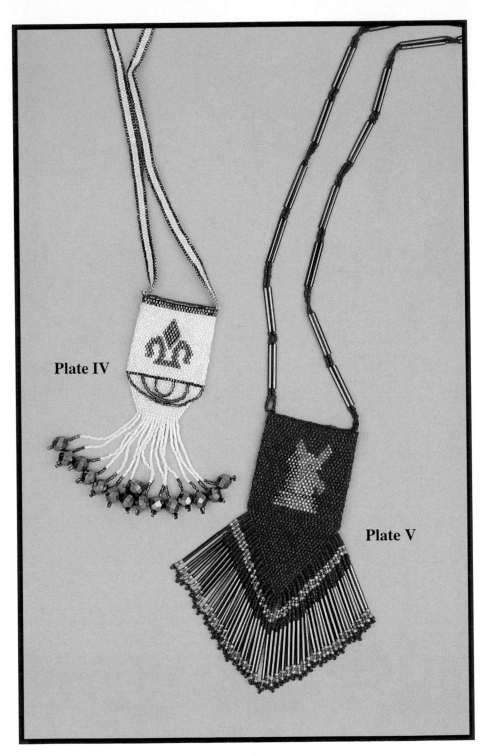

Plate IV

Plate V

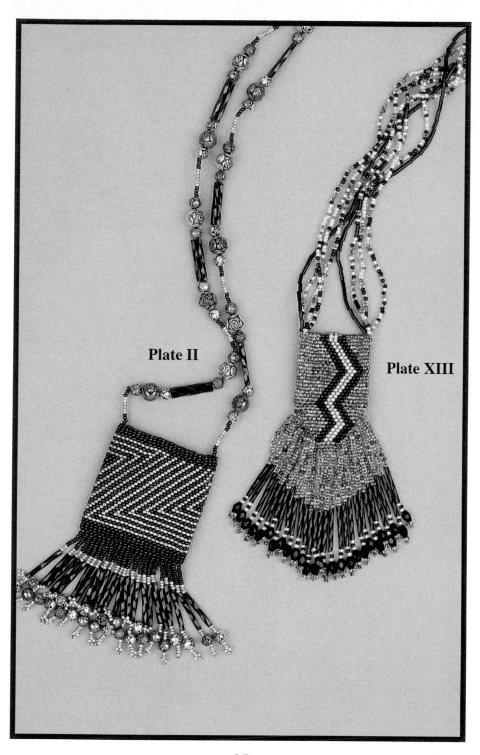

Plate II

Plate XIII

35

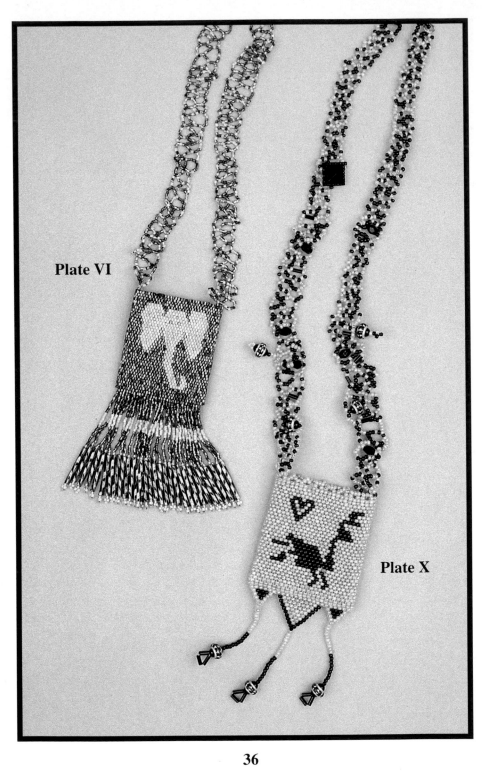

Plate VI

Plate X

36

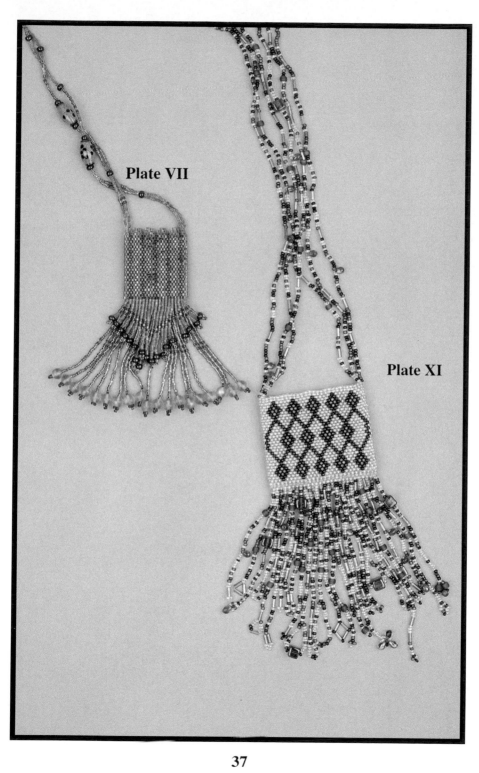

Plate VII

Plate XI

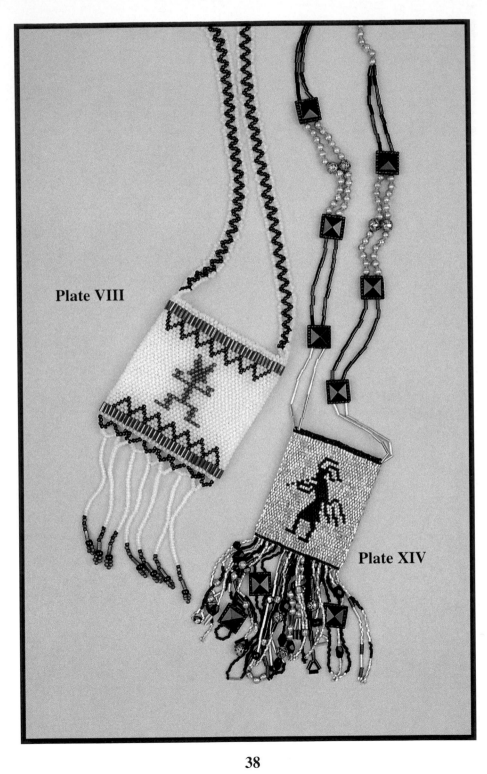

Plate VIII

Plate XIV

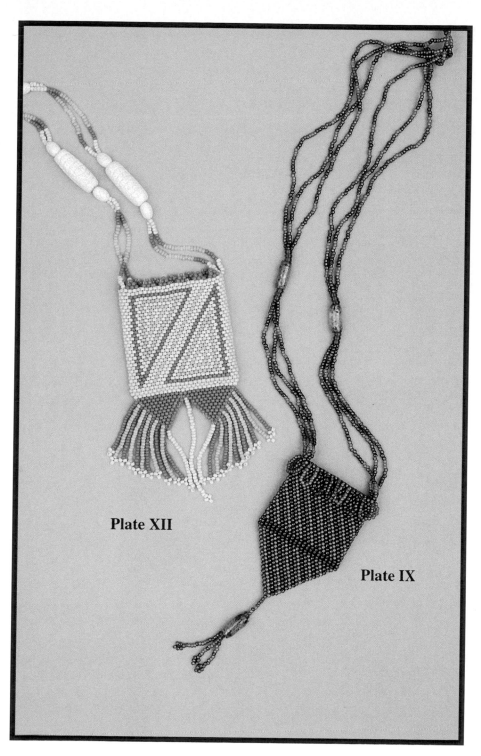

Plate XII

Plate IX

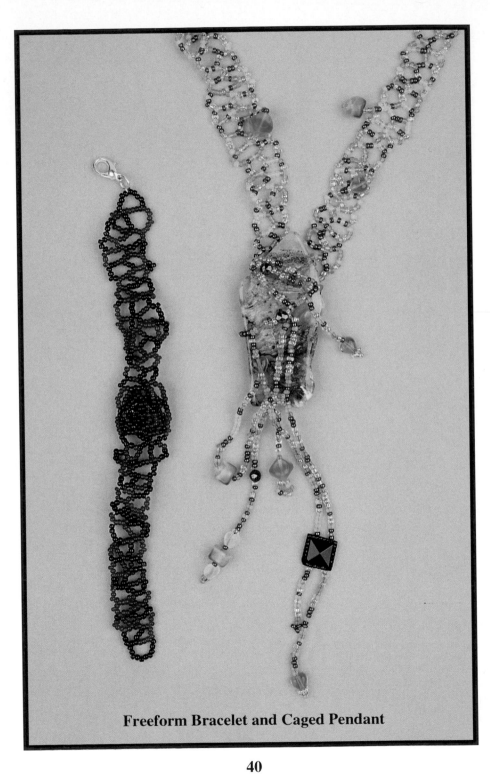

Freeform Bracelet and Caged Pendant

40

top to bottom, and then up through the last bead of this row from bottom to top (**Figure 28**).

When this row is completed - and do this for all other rows charted on the lines of the graph paper - place a "check" mark off to the right side of the chart to help keep your place.

The **Second Row** (and all even numbered rows above the foundation row) is charted in the spaces of the graph paper and the right edge bead is an "out" bead. Place a "minus" mark off to the right side of the chart when this row - and all other rows charted in the spaces - has been completed.

Follow the chart and complete this row all the way around to where the row began. When the beginning point is reached, **join this (and all even numbered or "out" bead rows)** by passing the needle

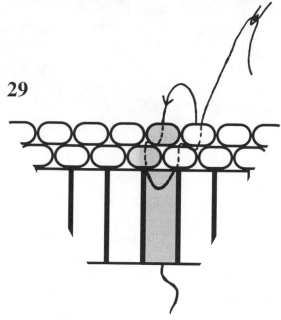

and thread down through the first bead of this row from top to bottom, and then down through the bead directly below and to the left of this bead, then up through the bead directly to the right of this bead (in the same row), then up through the first bead again (**Figure 29**). This places the needle and thread at the starting place of the next working row.

Continue working the remainder of the purse body using the method just described for the particular row being beaded.

By following these joining techniques, the starting point will

always begin at the right edge of the chart. This procedure will keep the starting place from spiraling around the beadwork, as will happen if the rows are joined only in the manner described for Row 1, and as happens in Tubular Peyote.

This joining and marking technique is very helpful in keeping your place, especially when the work must be set down and come back to later. The place to begin again on the chart can be determined immediately. Try it, it makes beading a purse much easier.

Complete the body of the purse by following the instructions above, joining the ends of each row as described, and proceeding to the next row. Follow the chart for the design until the top row is finished. Join this row together by passing the needle down through the first bead of this row, and up the last bead of this row (see Figure 28), then repeat this step again to reinforce the piece.

Tie a knot by passing the needle and thread (no beads on) under the span of thread between the beads next to where the thread exits, and pulling until a small loop remains. Pass the needle through this loop and pull up tight. Repeat this step, making another knot on top of the first knot. Hide the thread by working it into the beadwork and then cut the thread. Or, if the thread is long enough, work it down through the body of the purse, through beads along the side, finally passing the needle and thread through the bead(s) in the foundation row where the short tail of thread is found.

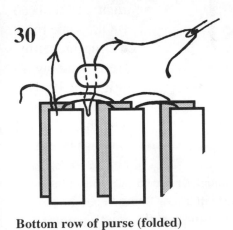

30

Bottom row of purse (folded)

To close the bottom of the purse, turn the purse upside down, and also turn the chart upside down. Hold the front and back sides of the purse together, lining up the two sides across from each other, and making sure the design is centered. (If this closing row is a part of the design, be sure to read the chart for proper bead color placement.) If necessary, start a new length of thread. Place a bead on the thread and pass the needle and thread under **both spans of thread** between the beads that are across from each other on the bottom of the purse. Take the needle and thread back through the bead just added, working as though the folded foundation row were a single row (**Figure 30**). Work all across this row in the same manner, placing a bead above each double span of thread. This row will close the bottom of the tube, making it a purse. When the closing row is completed, tie the thread off by working it through the piece as usual in brick stitch, or continue beading, finishing the purse with whatever details have been chosen. **Note:** When closing the bottom of the purse using brick stitch, the bead count in the closing row will decrease by one bead. This is important to remember if the design is included as part of the closing row.

TOP EDGE TRIMMINGS

Picot Edging

This edging is done with the working thread emerging out of the top of a bead in the top row of the purse. Begin on the right hand side with the front of the purse facing the beader. Add a new thread if necessary, as explained in the Basic Brick Stitch instructions (page 25). An example of Picot Edging can be seen on the Frills pattern given on page 64 and pictured on page 13.

Begin by placing 3 beads on the needle, and passing the needle and thread under the span of thread to the left, as is done in regular brick stitch. Pull the thread so that the beads are snug against the top of the bag. Pass the needle up through the last of the three beads just placed on the needle, going from bottom to top. This will form a small triangle of beads, with one bead sitting above and between the two beads below it. **From this point on, place only two beads on the needle at a time**. Continue around the purse, placing two beads on the needle, passing the needle and thread under the next span of thread (working right to left) and up through the last bead placed on the

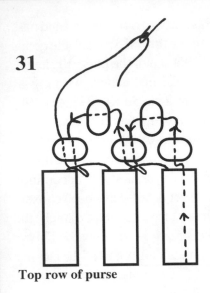

31

Top row of purse

needle, as was done in the prior step (**Figure 31**). Repeat these steps around the purse until the edging is completed. To finish the edging smoothly, it may be necessary to adjust the bead count when the place where the edging began is reached. When the top edging is complete, run the thread through some existing beads; follow the direction of the beading to make sure the thread is concealed. Tie two knots, run the thread through a few more beads and cut the thread.

Brick Stitch Points Edging

This edging is done with the working thread emerging from the top of a bead in the top row of the purse. Begin on the right hand side with the purse facing the beader. Add a new thread if necessary, as explained in the Basic Brick Stitch instructions (page 25). An example of Brick Stitch Points Edging can be seen on the Ribbons pattern shown on pages 70 and 71.

The brick stitch points can be any width desired. Generally three or four beads wide - per point - is sufficient for a small project such as a purse. For larger projects a wider point can be made.

For a point that is three beads wide at the bottom, begin by working a regular brick stitch until three beads have been added above the top row of the purse, working from right to left. Now working back across from left to right, add beads in a regular brick stitch above the two spans of thread that lie between the three beads just added. For the row above this (the top of the point), work one bead above the span of thread between the two beads just worked in the row below. When this point is complete, bring the needle and thread over the left edge of the top bead and down through the edge bead in each of the two rows below (**Figure 32**). Now bring the needle and thread down through the bead just below this bead (this bead will be in the top row of the purse body), and then up through the bead in the same row, just to the left of this bead (also in the top row of the purse body). The

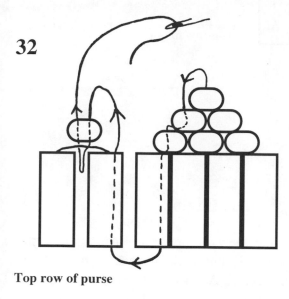

32

Top row of purse

needle and thread are now in place to make the next brick stitch point. Repeat the same steps as for the first point and continue repeating these same steps until there are brick stitch points all the way around the purse, or just across the front, or just across the back, if preferred. Tie the thread off in the usual manner.

Top Loops Edging

This edging is done with the working thread emerging from the bottom of a bead in the top row of the purse (count this bead as one). Begin on the left hand side with the purse facing the beader. Add a new thread if necessary, as explained in the Basic Brick Stitch instructions (page 25). An example of Top Loops Edging can be seen on the Stripes on the Diagonal purse pictured on Page 48.

Add the desired number of beads for a loop (15 on the Stripes on the Diagonal purse). The color(s) of beads in the loop are a matter of personal choice. Skip the next bead on the top row and pass the needle up through the third bead of the top row. Go down through the fourth bead (Figure **33**). The needle and thread are now in position to make the next loop. Repeat the same steps as for the first loop and continue

45

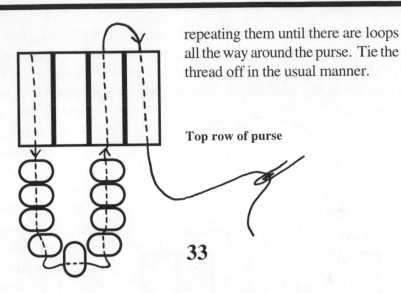

repeating them until there are loops all the way around the purse. Tie the thread off in the usual manner.

Top row of purse

33

Scallop Edging

This edging is done with the working thread emerging from the top of a bead in the top row of the purse. Begin on the right hand side with the purse facing the beader. Add a new thread if necessary, as explained in the Basic Brick Stitch instructions (page 25). An

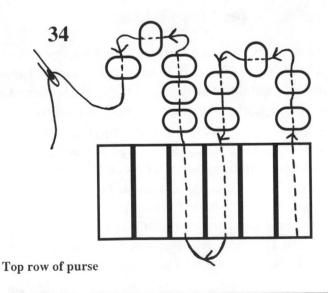

Top row of purse

example of Scallop Edging can be seen on the Deer To My Heart pattern shown on pages 74 and 75.

Add the desired number of beads for the first scallop to the thread (five on the Deer To My Heart purse). Do not use so many beads that the scallops are floppy. Skip the desired number of beads in the top row (one in the case of the Deer To My Heart Purse). Take the needle and thread down through the chosen bead in the top row of the purse, then up through the next bead to the left (also in the top row of the purse). This positions the needle and thread for making the next scallop (**Figure 34**). Continue around the purse, adding the same number of beads for each scallop and skipping the same number of beads between scallops. When the beginning point is reached, tie the thread off in the usual manner.

Fringe Dangle Edging

This edging is done with the working thread emerging from the bottom of a bead in the top row of the purse. Begin on the left hand side with the purse facing the beader. Add a new thread if necessary, as explained in the Basic Brick Stitch instructions (page 25).

Before deciding to add fringe around the top of the purse, be sure that it will not interfere with the design on the purse. If the design on the body of the purse reaches to the top portion, it may be better to not put fringe on the top edge of this piece. Fringe works very well on portions of the purse where there is no design that can be covered up, or on a purse that has a repeated pattern, such as diagonal stripes, where the portion of the design covered is the same as the portion that remains showing.

Place the desired number of beads on the needle in the sequence desired and, skipping the turn-around beads, attach the dangle in the same manner as is done on a foundation row in basic brick stitch (see Phase III, pages 19-21). Work from left to right and add the fringe dangles across the front of the purse; continue around the back of the purse if desired. Tie off the thread, conceal it in some of the beads in the purse body, and then cut the thread.

Stripes on the Diagonal

BOTTOM EDGE TRIMMINGS

Double-Beaded Bottom

After the upper (body) portion of the purse is completed, personal preference or the design may require that a bottom, double-beaded portion be added. That is, the bottom portion below the closing row of the purse will also be beaded using brick stitch. For details, please read the instructions for double-beaded brick stitch on pages 24-25.

Any number of rows may be included in this bottom portion. Viewing the photographs and charts in this book will show how the bottom portion of each purse that is double-beaded has been completed. Some purses have a few rows of brick stitch on the bottom, some have an entire brick stitch triangle as the bottom portion of the purse, and on some purses, there is more than one triangle section.

To work this portion, it is more convenient to turn the graph paper of the chart upside down, as the beadwork is done with the purse turned upside down. In fact, the beadwork and graph may already be upside down as a result of completing the closing row.

Hold the beadwork upside down, with the needle and thread on the right hand side. Follow the chart and work in the regular brick stitch method until the end of this portion is reached, then finish the purse as usual.

If a purse has a bottom section containing more than one brick stitch triangle, it is easier to bead each triangle entirely, before going on to the next triangle. When one triangle is complete, work the needle and thread down through this triangle to its base, and then work sideways through the beads to the place where the next triangle is to begin. Do this for each triangle portion added.

When the bottom double-beaded portion is complete, add fringe dangles if they are desired. If the thread is rather short, tie the working thread off and start a new piece of thread in the regular manner.

Fringe Dangle Bottom Edging

Bottom fringe can be added to the purses if desired, and can be used as sparingly as one tassel, or as full and lavish as desired. Any type of bead can be used in the fringe - the same small beads used in the purse, small and large millimeter beads combined, charms or fetishes, porcupine quills, pieces of bone or horn, etc. Fringe can also be made using only accent beads and very few or none of the small beads used in the purse. Keep in mind that beads that are too large will detract from the purse and may interfere with the fringe hanging properly if used too extensively.

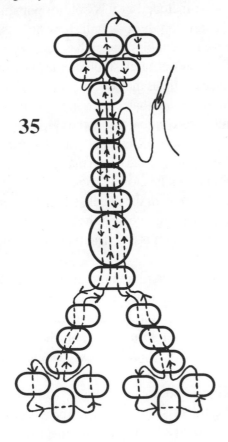

35

In adding fringe, starting at the bottom left side of the purse and working across from left to right is most convenient, as the beads already added are out of the way as the fringe progresses. The thread should be coming out of the bottom of the bead where the first dangle is to be added. The bead dangles are added in the same way as for Basic Brick Stitch (see Phase III, pages 19-21). When the fringe is complete tie the thread in two knots, conceal the thread through some beads and cut the thread.

To add a single tassel dangle, work the thread through the beadwork, so that the working thread is coming out of the bottom of the bead where the tassel is to hang. Add the desired number of beads for the main part of the tassel, including a larger accent bead. Skip the turn around beads and work back up through the tassel to the starting place.

The tassel effect is created by adding more than one fringe element below the accent bead in the main dangle (**Figure 35**). Work the thread through a few beads in the section above the main tassel, then go down through the tassel and through the accent bead. The thread is now in position to add an extra fringe element. Add the beads for this element, skip the turn around beads, and work back up through the element beads as well as through the main tassel beads. Repeat these steps until the desired number of elements has been added. Work the thread back through the body of the beadwork and finish off as usual. An example of a single tassel dangle can be seen in the picture of the Stripes on the Diagonal design on page 48.

Netted Fringe Edging

To begin a netted fringe, start on the left hand side with the front of the purse towards the beader. The working thread should be coming out the bottom of the first bead of the closing row of the purse (for details on the closing row, see pages 42-43). An example of Netted Fringe Edging can be seen in the picture of the Spring Man design on page 30. This example is used for these instructions, but variations in the number of beads added or skipped are possible. Put

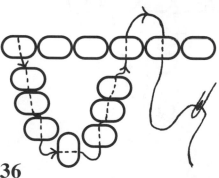

36

7 dark beads on the thread, skip the next two beads in the closing row, and pass the needle and thread up through the fourth bead in the closing row. Now go down through the next bead in the closing row, ready to add the next set of

beads (**Figure 36**). Repeat this sequence across to the right side of the purse.

Note: For an evenly spaced netting row, the closing row must be divisible by the number of beads used to anchor each "net", i.e. if the first and fourth beads are used to anchor the net (4 beads total), then the closing row must be divisible by 4. The Spring Man design has 32 beads on the closing row, and using 4 anchor beads per "net" results in 8 evenly spaced "nets" (32 divided by 4 = 8 "nets").

To begin the second row of netting, pass the needle and thread (no beads on the thread) up through the foundation bugle bead on the right edge of the purse (just above where the needle and thread exits the closing row). Go down through the next bugle bead to the left and continue down through the first bead on the right side of the closing row. Then go down through 4 of the dark beads on the right side of the last (right hand) net. Pick up 7 light beads and working from right to left, pass the needle and thread through the center bead of the next net in the previous row (**Figure 37**). Add 7 more light beads to the thread and go through the center bead of the next dark net to the left. Continue in this way across to the left side of the purse. **Note:** The

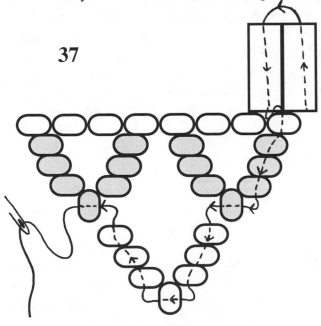

37

number of "nets" decreases by one net per row.

To finish the second row, pass the needle and thread up through the 4 dark beads on the left side of the left hand net and continue up through the left edge bead of the closing row. Go around the outside edge of this same bead, and back down through the left 4 beads of the dark net and the left 3 beads of the light net just below. Place the desired number and combination of beads for the first fringe on the needle and thread. Skip the turn around beads and go up through the dangle as usual. Then go through the 3 light beads on the right side of this same net (bypassing the center bead), and through the center dark bead of the net above. Go down through 3 beads on the left side of the next light net, ready to add the next fringe (**Figure 38**).

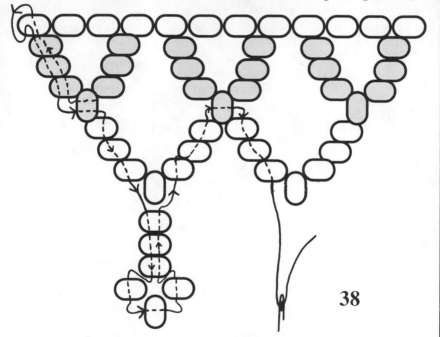

38

Continue across to the right side, repeating these steps for a total of 7 dangles. Run the needle and thread up through the 3 light beads and 4 dark beads of the right side nets and into the closing row. Tie off and hide the thread in the body of the purse, then cut off the remaining thread.

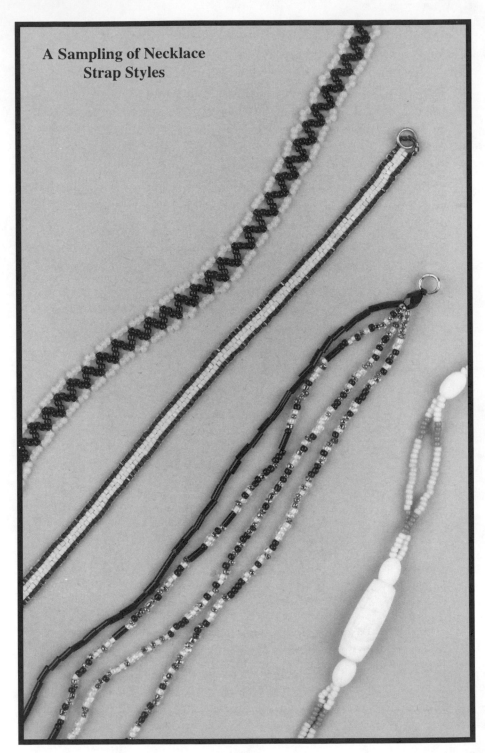

A Sampling of Necklace
Strap Styles

NECKLACE STRAPS

Strand Purse Straps

To make single strand necklace straps, start by attaching a new thread. Conceal it in a portion of the existing beadwork, with the point of exit being a bead on the top row of the purse, at the position where the strap will hang. Place the desired number of beads on the thread, in a pattern sequence if desired, until the proper length for the strap is reached. Attach any findings at this point (clasps, jump rings, etc.) by wrapping the thread around the finding loop several times. Make sure the beads remain snug on the thread as the findings are added. Return the thread back through all the strap beads to the beginning point and secure the end in the beadwork of the purse.

Additional strands may be worked on the same side, repeating the steps above until the desired number of strands is reached. Use the same procedure for the strands on the opposite side of the purse. If there is a definite pattern sequence in the strands, the same pattern should be repeated on both sides of the purse so that they will match. A patterned sequence is not, however, necessary - strands can be made by picking up beads at random.

Multiple strands can also be made by running shorter sections of bead strands through "station" beads put in place when making the first strand. After the first strand is strung, place the proper number of beads on each additional strand to reach the first station bead. Run the thread through the station bead, and continue adding sections of beads between station beads until the strand is complete.

There are many Strand Straps on the purses pictured in this book. Look at the photographs for examples and use them as springboards for new ideas.

Flat Peyote Straps

This is only a brief explanation of flat peyote stitch. As this solid color strap with a border is worked, the beader will become familiar with the flat peyote stitch and, by observing how the beads lay, can begin to understand how to lay in patterns.

This flat peyote strap is an even-count, 4-bead-wide band. Notice however, that to begin such an even-count band, an uneven number of beads are picked up on the thread. The #5 bead is the same color as the edge border beads (#1 and #4) because it becomes an edge border bead and falls into place as the weaving is begun. An example of this strap can be seen on the Fleur-de-lis purse pictured on Page 61.

To begin, attach the thread to the purse by concealing it in a portion of the existing beadwork. The point of exit should be a bead on the top row of the purse, at the position where the strap will begin.

Place on the needle: 1 dark (#1), 2 light (# 2 and #3), and 2 dark (# 4 and #5) beads. With the short tail of thread on the left, skip beads #5 and #4 (dark) and pass the needle through #3 (light) as shown in **Figure 39**. Add 1 light bead (#6) and pass the needle through bead #1 (dark) from right to left (**Figure 40**).

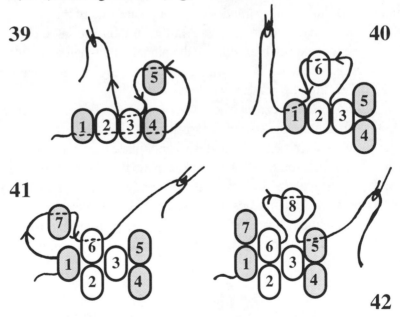

Add 1 dark bead (#7) and pass the needle from left to right through bead #6 (light) as shown in **Figure 41**. Add 1 light bead (#8) and pass the needle from left to right through bead #5 (dark; **Figure 42**). Add 1 dark bead (#9) and pass the needle from right to left through bead #8 (light). Add one light bead (#10) and pass the thread from right to left through bead #7 (dark; **Figure 43**). Continue in this manner, as shown in **Figure 44**, working back and forth across the piece until the desired length is reached.

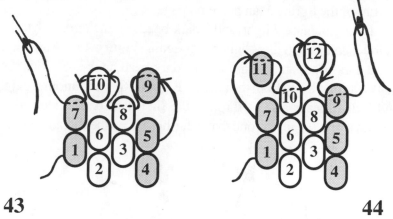

43   **44**

This strap can be made in two halves (divided) or as a single continuous strap. When the desired length for a divided strap is reached, attach the appropriate findings (clasp, jump rings, etc.), using a reinforced loop of beads between the two edges of the strap. Then tie the thread off by working it through some of the beads in the strap, tying two knots on the edge of the strap, and running the needle and thread through more beads in the strap. Cut the thread. Complete the second side of the strap in exactly the same manner.

A continuous strap reaches from one side of the purse to the opposite side with no findings involved. Make sure the strap is long enough to fit over the head with no difficulty. Attach the strap to the opposite side of the purse by running the needle and thread through some of the beads in the body of the purse and then back through some of the beads in the strap. Tie the thread off on the edge of the strap, run it through a few more beads of the strap to conceal the end and cut the thread.

Chevron Chains

It is easiest to make this strap separately and then attach it to the purse. The strap can be a continuous one that fits over the head of the wearer, or, two separate chains can be made and a clasp attached to the two loose ends to fasten the strap. An example can be seen in the picture of the Spring Man purse on page 30.

To begin, place 7 light, and 3 dark beads on the thread. Making a circle, go through the 7 light beads again (**Figure 45**). Add 3 light and 3 dark beads and go through the dark bead, in the previous row, that is farthest away from the needle (**Figure 46**). Add another 3 light and 3 dark beads and go through the first dark bead added in the previous row (again the one that is farthest from the threads point of origin).

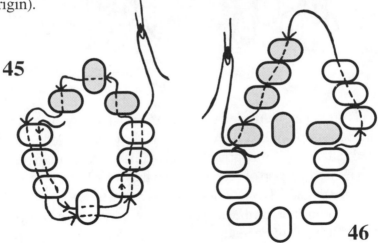

45

46

Continue adding 3 light and 3 dark beads in this same pattern until the desired length is reached (**Figure 47**). **Note:** Each time beads are added, the bead that the needle passes through will be on the opposite side of the chain from the point where the needle and thread originates. In other words, the work will be from right to left, to right, etc. in a zig-zag, back-and-forth fashion each time beads are added.

Figure 48 shows that the interior (dark) beads of the chain

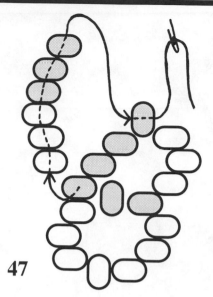

47

actually turn and lie at an angle to the outer (light) beads in the chain.

End the chain with a loop of 7 light beads, to match the beginning loop. Tie a knot between two beads and run the thread back through a few beads to hide the end. Cut the thread. Do the same with the thread at the beginning of the chain. This stitch can also be used to make bracelets, strips for barrettes, strips for clothing, and other decorations.

To attach the Chevron chain to the purse, choose the desired strap location and weave the needle and thread (with no beads on the thread) through several beads in the purse and then through several beads in the strap. Repeat this two or three times for strength. Tie the thread off between beads. Hide the thread in several more beads and cut the thread.

Repeat this procedure on the other side of the purse, lining up the two strap attachment points, so the piece will hang evenly. **Note:** Make sure the strap does not twist while it or the findings (if desired) are being attached.

48

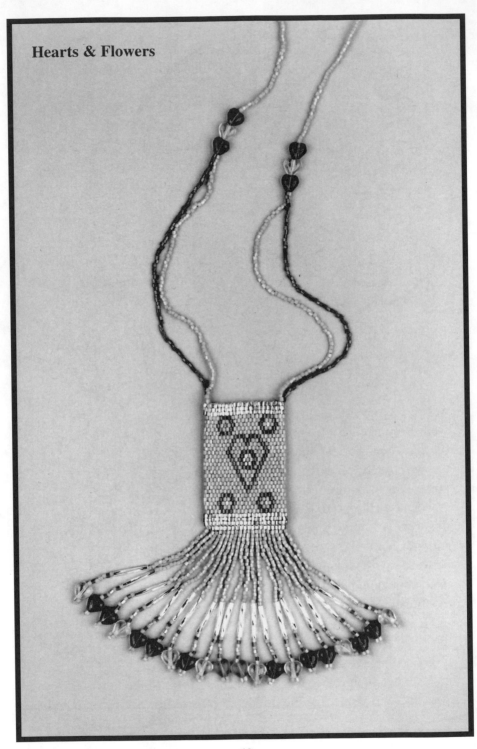

TREASURE PURSE DESIGNS

The following pages contain graphs of designs for making tubular brick stitch purses, using the techniques outlined in the preceding sections. Variations may be made in any of the graphed designs by changing colors or the type of bead used. The addition of different top and/or bottom edgings, or purse straps will also personalize the purse greatly.

On all these graphs, the symbol **F** is used to designate the foundation row and the symbol **C** designates the closing row of the purse. **Note**: The design on page 78 was derived from the wallpaper on the bathroom wall at a hotel. It is named after "room 421". There are a vast number of places for design ideas - just look for them.

Fleur-de-lis

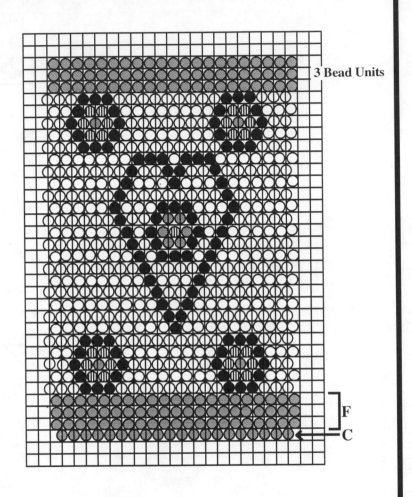

3 Bead Units

F
C

Plate I
Hearts & Flowers
Hexagon Beads (Total Foundation: 21 x 2 = 42)

- ◉ Silver
- ○ Dusty Pink
- ● Plum
- ⦷ Hot Pink

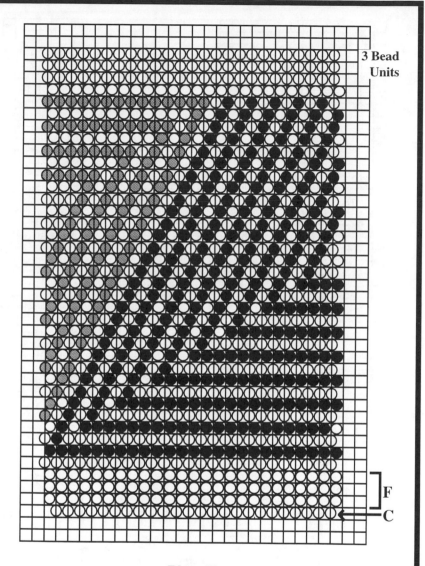

3 Bead Units

F
C

Plate II
"Z" Purse
Size 11/° Beads (Total Foundation: 25 x 2 = 50)

○ Dark Blue Iris

● Silver

◉ Gold

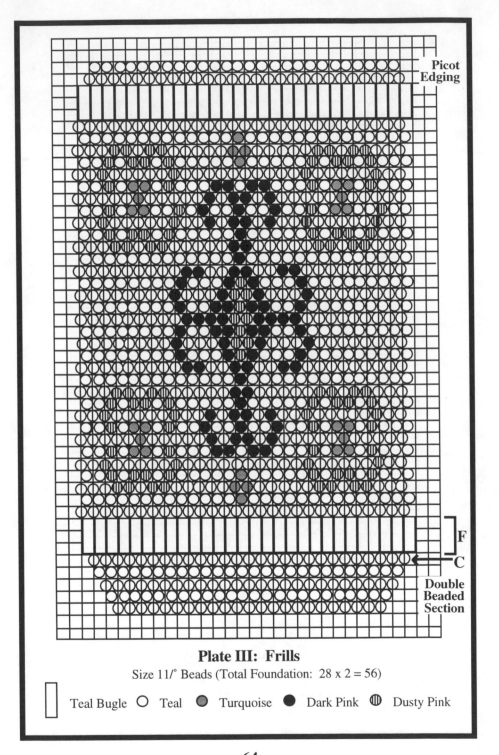

Plate III: Frills

Size 11/° Beads (Total Foundation: 28 x 2 = 56)

☐ Teal Bugle ○ Teal ◉ Turquoise ● Dark Pink ⦷ Dusty Pink

64

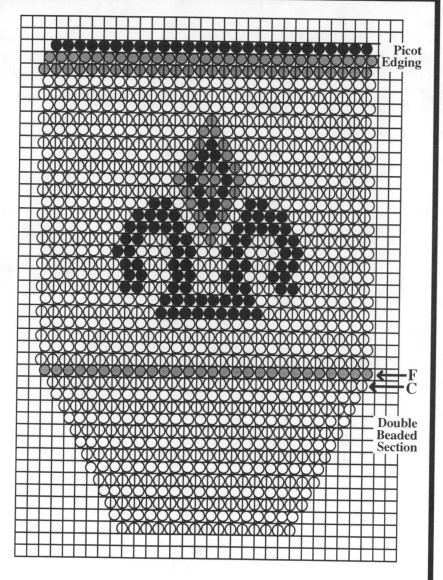

Picot Edging

←F
←C

Double Beaded Section

Plate IV: Fleur-de-lis
Delica Beads (Total Foundation: 28 x 2 = 56)

● Copper-Orange

○ Ivory

◉ Bronze

Plate V: Windmill
Size 12/°, 3-Cut Beads (Total Foundation: 28 x 2 = 56)

○	Red
●	Amber
◉	Light Blue
◫	Dark Blue

66

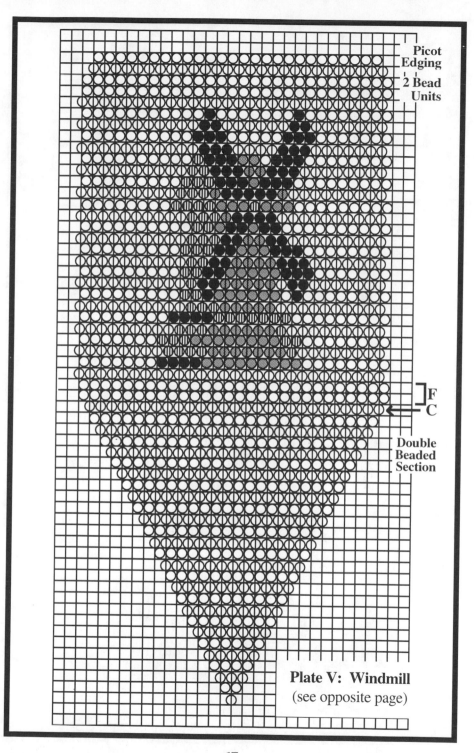

Picot
Edging
2 Bead
Units

F
C

Double
Beaded
Section

Plate V: Windmill
(see opposite page)

Hairy Elephante'

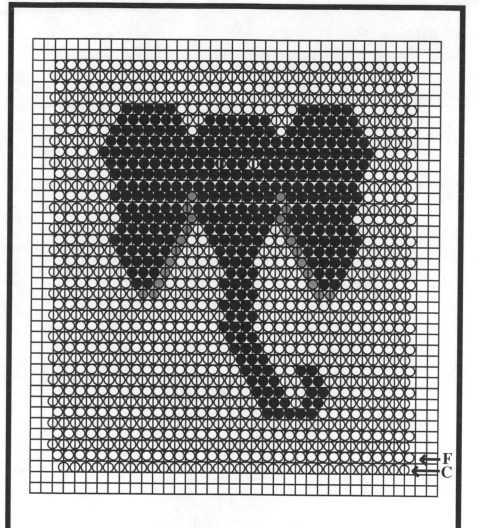

Plate VI
Hairy Elephante'

Hexagon Beads (Total Foundation: 33 x 2 = 66)

O	Gun Metal
●	Grey
◐	Gold
◑	Black

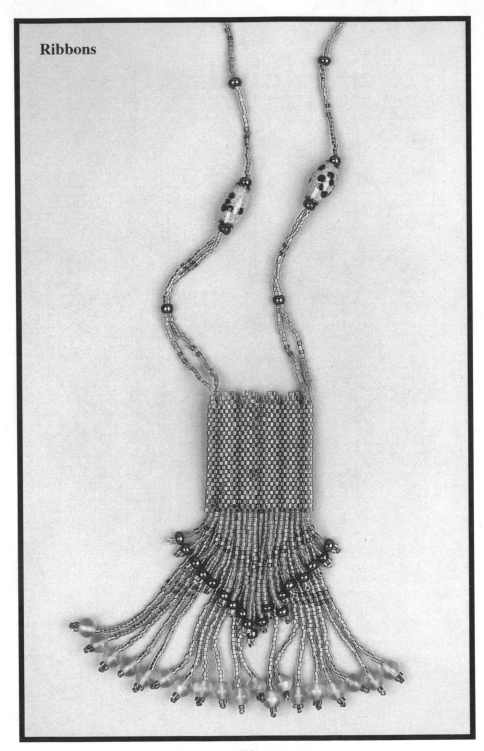

Ribbons

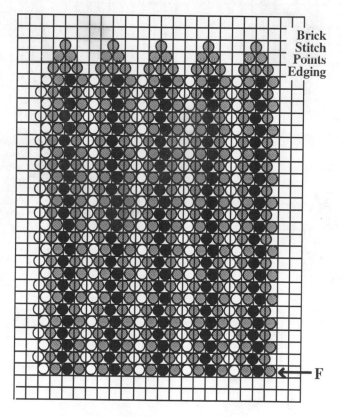

Brick Stitch Points Edging

← F

Plate VII
Ribbons

Delica Beads (Total Foundation: 20 x 2 = 40)

- ○   Luster Cobalt
- ●   Lined Magenta AB
- ◉   Grey

Note: The bottom closing on this bag was done by whip-stitching the front and back together, with no beads on the thread. This allows the placement of fringe on the front and back rows of the bag.

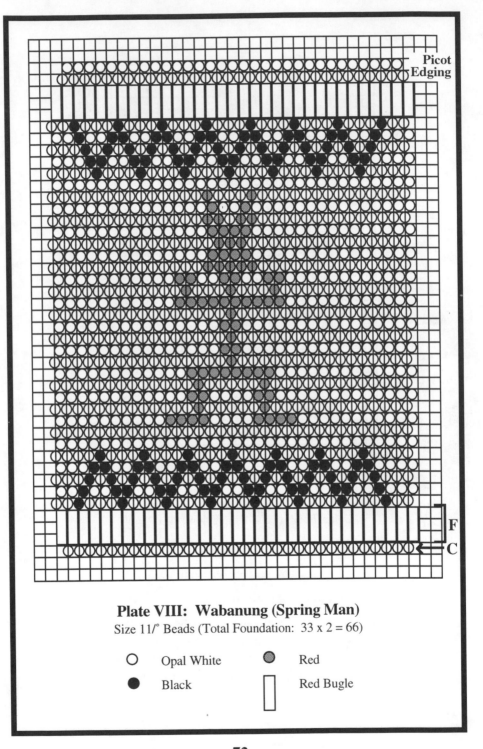

Plate VIII: Wabanung (Spring Man)

Size 11/° Beads (Total Foundation: 33 x 2 = 66)

O	Opal White	◉	Red
●	Black	▯	Red Bugle

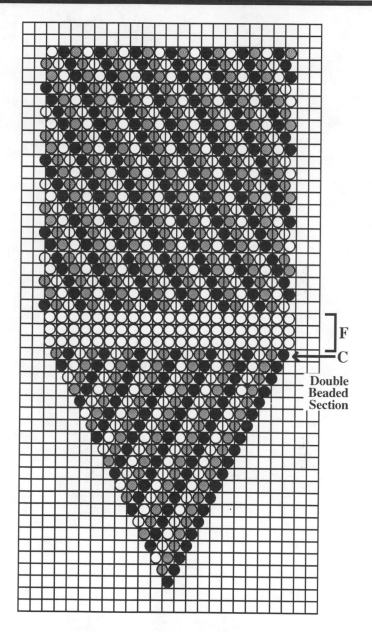

Plate IX: Stripes on the Diagonal

Size 11/° Beads (Total Foundation: 21 x 2 = 42)

○ Bronze ● Mauve ● Dark Green

73

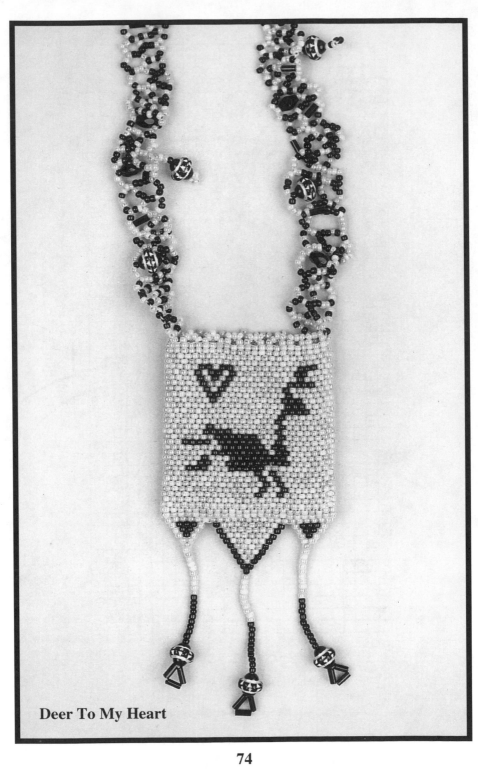

Deer To My Heart

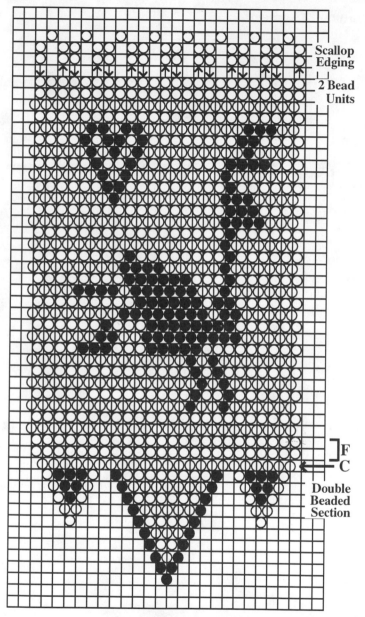

Scallop
Edging

2 Bead
Units

F
C

Double
Beaded
Section

Plate X: Deer To My Heart

Size 11/° Beads (Total Foundation: 24 x 2 = 48)

○ Grey Pearl   ● Black

Diamond Connection

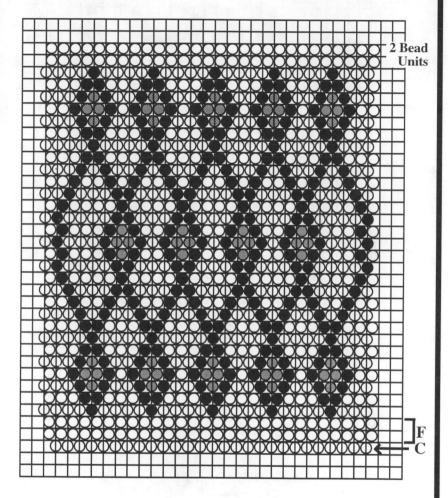

2 Bead
Units

F
C

Plate XI
Diamond Connection

Size 11/° Beads (Total Foundation: 28 x 2 = 56)

○   Lavender Iris

●   Purple Metallic Iris

◍   Brown Frost

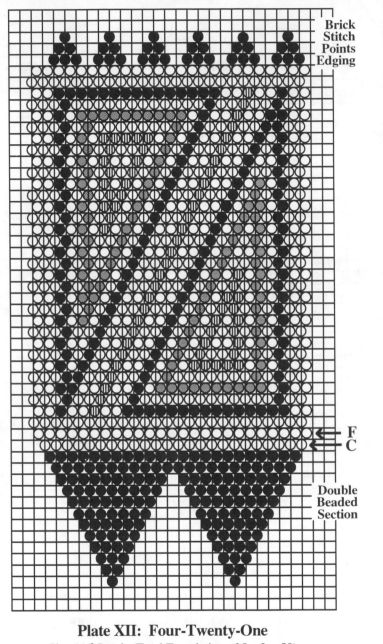

Brick
Stitch
Points
Edging

F
C

Double
Beaded
Section

Plate XII: Four-Twenty-One
Size 11/° Beads (Total Foundation: 25 x 2 = 50)

○ Ivory   ◉ Flesh   ● Tan   ⦀ Green

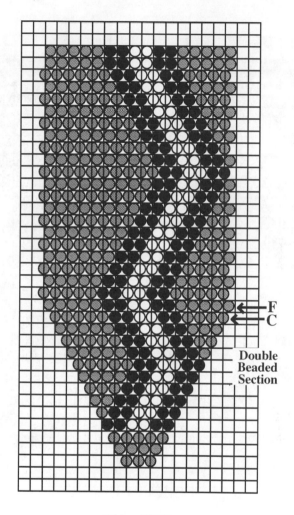

F
C

**Double
Beaded
Section**

Plate XIII
Zig-Zags
Size 11/° Beads (Total Foundation: 16 x 2 =32)

○   Crystal Iris

●   Black

◓   Gunmetal Iris

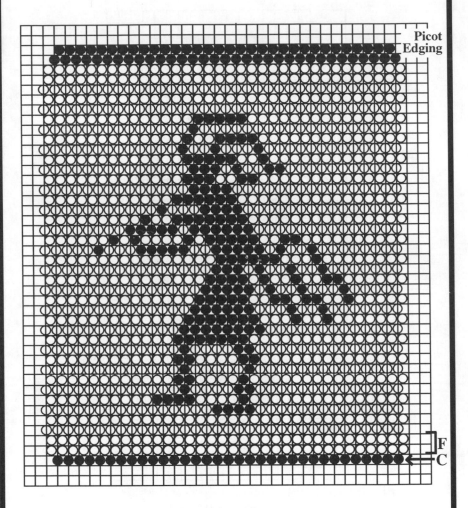

Plate XIV
Kokopelli
Hexagon Beads (Total Foundation: 34 x 2 = 68)

○   Gold

●   Black

FREEFORM STITCH

INSTRUCTIONS

To describe the freeform stitch is a bit awkward as it is just as the name implies, "free of form". This stitch is lovely because it is a refreshing deviation from having to follow any chart or design pattern - the beader just goes with the flow. Choose any type of bead, or combination, and use them as the spirit dictates - mixed, matched, big, small, seed, bugle, hex, delica - it doesn't really matter. The more beaders play with this stitch, the more most of them grow to love it. It is fun, fun, fun, and it enhances the more formal forms of beadwork because of its contrast; it will also enhance the more contemporary and even traditional styles of beadwork.

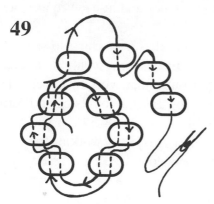

49

Begin by placing a few beads on the needle; specific number isn't important, but experiment with from four to eight beads at first. Join the beads into a ring by running the needle and thread through all of the beads a second time, and then go through the first bead a third time.

After the ring is formed, choose and place a number of beads on the needle and thread. Skip one bead in the ring and pass the needle and thread through the next bead on the ring (**Figure 49**). Pull the thread up snug. Place more beads of choice on the needle, skip one bead on the ring and pass the needle and thread through the next bead. This creates loops around the initial ring.

Note: The more beads used on the needle at one time, the lacier and more open the beadwork will be. Therefore, if a more closely woven look is preferred in freeform, use fewer beads - even as few as one at a time - in the weaving. Look at the photographs of the pieces in this book where freeform was used to see what is meant by lacier and more open, as opposed to more closely woven. Feel free to add any accent beads where desired, in among the smaller beads being used. This will give the beadwork a more textured look, rather than a look that is smooth and flat. When adding larger millimeter beads, using a few of the smaller beads on each side of the large accent bead will make it lay better.

To make a circular piece, which works well for earrings, brooches, pendants and other small pieces, make loops all the way around the beginning ring. Then, with no beads on the needle, pass the needle and thread through the first loop made until the center portion of the loop is reached. From this position, make a second row of loops around the row of loops just completed.

When this second row is finished, continue (if desired) to make additional rows of loops in the same manner, adding a few more beads as the rows progress outward.

Straight pieces, such as straps, bracelets, etc., can also be made using freeform. To start a straight piece, form a ring as already described for a circular piece. Then, rather than working in a circular motion around that ring, work in a zig-zag motion, back and forth across the piece (the Chevron Strap on pages 58-59 is a patterned version of this concept). However, the two styles of working freeform (circular and zig-zag) can be combined in the same piece. Let imagination be the guiding light.

Texture can be added to a piece by building on top of the beadwork already done. This is accomplished by adding additional bead strands in a layered, 3-dimensional fashion. Place the selected beads on the thread, lay them on top of the previously beaded section, and pass the needle through existing beads in this section. When the desired amount of texture has been added to a section, continue on with the freeform. If more texture is desired in a certain section, work the thread back to the appropriate place and add more beads. Just

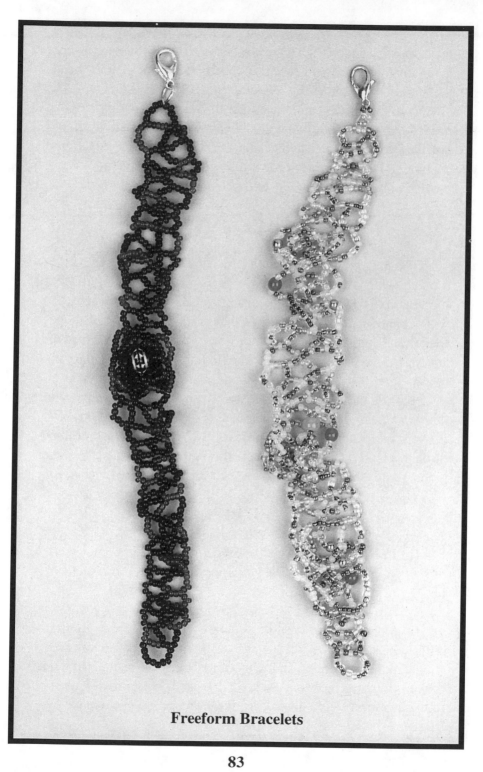

Freeform Bracelets

make sure that enough beads are used to reach across the span and not leave any thread showing, and also that there are not so many beads that the strand becomes too long and flops over the side.

When the piece is completed, tie the thread off by passing the needle under the thread that lies between two beads in the work, and pull the thread through leaving a loop. Then pass the needle through the loop and pull up tight to form a knot. Repeat a second time. Work the thread back through a few beads and cut the thread.

BRACELETS

To make a bracelet, start with a rosette-type circle for the center section. This is done by forming a ring and then working rows of loops around the ring until this center piece is the desired size. To work a band for a bracelet, follow the directions for making a straight section and complete one side of the bracelet band. Tie the thread off and finish in the regular manner. The finding for this side of the band (clasp, jump ring, etc.) may be added before cutting the thread.

To begin the other side of the bracelet band, add a new piece of thread where the band is to be placed (see page 25). Tie the thread in between two beads at this point, making two knots, and run the thread through a few beads (2 or 3). Make this half of the band in the same manner as the band completed for the other side of the bracelet.

CAGED PIECES

The freeform stitch can also be used to "cage" a stone, glass piece, driftwood, etc. to form a pendant for a necklace, brooch, bracelet, bola tie, earrings, barrette, etc.

To cage a piece with beads, start by making a strand of beads that will fit around the piece in either direction - vertically or horizontally. Adjust the strand so that it fits nicely around the piece to be caged, snugly, but not too tight, and without any thread showing. Run the thread through all the beads a second time, and then through a portion of the first few beads a third time. It may be necessary to make two

Freeform Necklace with Caged Petrified Wood Pendant and Matching Freeform Earring

or more strands in this manner to secure the piece enough so that it can be worked on without it slipping out of the strands. Sometimes it is helpful to work a strand or so in each direction around the piece. Accent beads can be added at any place along the strands.

While working the strands around the piece it is easier to add additional strands by stringing just enough beads on the thread to reach the place where the strands intersect. From here, two methods may be used. For the first method, run the thread - with no beads on it - under the existing strand and continue to add beads to the working section of thread. The second method is to run the needle and thread through a few beads on the strand already in place, and then continue on with the working strand. This second method will add some interest to the piece and it will help in changing direction.

When the piece is caged satisfactorily, dangles can be added if they are desired. Simply work the thread into the beads at the place where the first dangle is wanted and add it using the regular method (see pages 19-21). Work the thread to the starting point for the second dangle and continue in the same manner. String the dangles in a random design to conform to the freeform style, or, for a more formal look, count the beads in each dangle so that the dangles hang uniformly in a pattern.

When the pendant is complete, the thread can be attached at any place on the pendant piece for a strap or attachment loop to be worked. Place these so that the piece will hang evenly when being worn. A freeform necklace strap works very well to compliment a piece worked in the freeform stitch.

Don't be intimidated by these instructions. They are not really specific, but freeform is just that - not really specific - it is a very unique stitch that can really bring out the creativity in a beader if they just let it happen. Therefore, there are no definite, rigid instructions. Again, refer to the photographs in the book and study them for ideas on making interesting freeform pieces. Many different looks can be accomplished using this stitch. **Have fun and experiment**!

SOME EAGLE'S VIEW PUBLISHING
BEST SELLERS THAT MAY BE OF INTEREST:

The Technique of Porcupine Quill Decoration Among the Indians of North America by W. C. Orchard (B00/01)	$8.95
The Technique of North American Indian Beadwork by Monte Smith (B00/02)	$10.95
Techniques of Beading Earrings by Deon DeLange (B00/03)	$7.95
More Techniques of Beading Earrings by Deon DeLange (B00/04)	$8.95
America's *First* First World War: The French and Indian War by Tim Todish (B00/05)	$8.95
Crow Indian Beadwork by Wildschut & Ewers (B00/06)	$8.95
New Adventures in Beading Earrings by Laura Reid (B00/07)	$8.95
North American Indian Burial Customs by Dr. H. C. Yarrow (B00/09)	$9.95
Traditional Indian Crafts by Monte Smith (B00/10)	$9.95
Traditional Indian Bead and Leather Crafts by M. Smith & M. VanSickle (B00/11)	$9.95
Indian Clothing of the Great Lakes: 1740-1840 by Sheryl Hartman (B00/12)	$10.95
Shinin' Trails: A Possibles Bag of Fur Trade Trivia by John Legg (B00/13)	$7.95
Adventures in Creating Earrings by Laura Reid (B00/14)	$9.95
A Circle of Power by William Higbie (B00/15)	$7.95
Etienne Provost: Man of the Mountains by Jack Tykal (B00/16)	$9.95
A Quillwork Companion by Jean Heinbuch (B00/17)	$9.95
Making Indian Bows & Arrows ... The Old Way by Doug Wallentine (B00/18)	$10.95
Making Arrows ... The Old Way by Doug Wallentine (B00/19)	$4.50
Hair of the Bear: Campfire Yarns and Stories by Eric Bye (B00/20)	$9.95
How to Tan Skins the Indian Way by Evard Gibby (B00/21)	$4.50
A Beadwork Companion by Jean Heinbuch (B00/22)	$10.95
Beads and Cabochons: Create Fashion Jewelry and Earrings by Patricia Lyman (B00/23)	$9.95
Earring Designs by Sig: Book I by Sigrid Wynne-Evans (B00/24)	$8.95
Creative Crafts by Marj by Marj Schneider (B00/25)	$9.95
How To Bead Earrings by Lori S. Berry (B00/26)	$10.95

SOME EAGLE'S VIEW PUBLISHING
BEST SELLERS THAT MAY BE OF INTEREST:

Delightful Beaded Earring Designs by Jan Radford (B00/27)	$8.95
Earring Designs by Sig II by Sigrid Wynne-Evans (B00/28)	$8.95
Craft Cord Corral by Janice S. Ackerman (B00/30)	$8.95
Classic Earring Designs by Nola May (B00/32)	$9.95
How To Make Primitive Pottery by Evard Gibby (B00/33)	$8.95
Plains Indian and Mountain Man Arts and Crafts by Charles W. Overstreet (B00/34)	$13.95
Beaded Images: Intricate Brick Stitch by Barbara Elbe (B00/35)	$9.95
Earring Designs by Sig III: Celebrations by Sigrid Wynne Evans (B00/36)	$9.95
Techniques of Fashion Earrings by Deon DeLange (B00/37)	$9.95
Beaded Images II: Intricate Brick Stitch Designs by Barbara Elbe (B00/38)	$9.95
Picture Beaded Earrings For Beginners by Starr Steil (B00/39)	$9.95
Plains Indian and Mountain Man Arts and Crafts II by Charles Overstreet (B00/40)	$12.95
Simple Lace & Other Beaded Jewelry Patterns by Mary Ellen Harte (B00/41)	$6.95
Beaded Treasure Purses: Tubular Brick Stitch Designs by Deon DeLange (B00/42)	$10.95
Eagle's View Publishing Catalog of Books	**$2.00**

• •
At your local bookstore or use this handy ordering form:
• •

Eagle's View Readers Service, Dept. BTP
6756 North Fork Road - Liberty, UT 84310

Please send me the titles listed. I am enclosing $_____
(Please add $3.50 per order to cover shipping and handling.)
Send check or money order - no cash or C.O.D.s please.

Ms./Mrs./Mr. _____

Address _____

City/State/Zip Code _____

Prices and availability subject to change without notice. Please allow
three to four weeks for delivery. (BTP -1/97)